Sebco
25.99

Mysterious Monsters

SEARCHING FOR THE YETI

JENNIFER RIVKIN

PowerKiDS press

New York

Published in 2015 by The Rosen Publishing Group, Inc.
29 East 21st Street, New York, NY 10010

Produced for Rosen by BlueApple*Works* Inc.
Art Director: Tibor Choleva
Designer: Joshua Avramson
Photo Research: Jane Reid
Editor for BlueApple*Works*: Melissa McClellan
US Editor: Joshua Shadowens

Illustrations: Cover , p. 1, 8–9 bottom, 10–11, 21, 22, 24-25 T. Choleva; p. 4–5, 15 top Carlyn Iverson; p. 29 right Mustafa

Photo Credits: Cover background Microstock Man /Shutterstock; p. 1 top Volodymyr Goinyk /Shutterstock; p. 6 top Honza
Hruby/Shutterstock; p. 6 middle, 28 top Daniel Prudek/Shutterstock; p 6–7 background Dmitry Pichugin/Dreamstime;
p. 7, 15 right Zzvet/Shutterstock; p. 8 top Roman Mikhailiuk/Shutterstock; p. 9 Brigida Soriano/Shutterstock; p. 10 top
Antonio Abrignani/Shutterstock; p. 10 Csaba Vanyi/Shutterstock; p. 12 top, 28–29 bottom Arsgera/Shutterstock; p. 12–13
background Gaman Mihai-Radu/Shutterstock; p. 12 Popperfoto/Getty Images; p. 13 roibu/Shutterstock; p. 14 top Zzvet/
Dreamstime; p. 14, 18, 26 Fortean Picture Library; p. 15 left Steve Estvanik/Shutterstock; p. 16 top Vronska/Shutterstock;
p. 16 Keystone Press; p 16–17 background AntonSokolov/Shutterstock; p. 17 TimofKingsland/Public Domain; p. 18 top
wavebreakmedia/Shutterstock; p. 19 Zuberka/Dreamstime; p. 20 top angellodeco/Shutterstock; p. 20-21 background
Jakub Cejpek/Shutterstock; p. 20 Pablo Utrilla/Dreamstime; p. 22 top Natalia Davidovich/Shutterstock; p. 23 R.M. Nunes/
Shutterstock; p. 23 right Cosmopolyt/Dreamstime; p. 24 top Nico Smit/Dreamstime; p. 24 Erik Mandre/Shutterstock; p. 25
left Catmando/Shutterstock; p. 25, 27 Marcio Silva/Dreamstime; p. 26 top, background Snehit/Shutterstock; p. 28 top inset
volkova natalia/Shutterstock; p. 28 left Granitepeaker/Dreamstime; p. 28 right saiko3p/Shutterstock; paper background
Fedorov Oleksiy/Shutterstock

Library of Congress-in-Publication Data

Rivkin, Jennifer, author.
  Searching for the Yeti / by Jennifer Rivkin.
      pages cm. — (Mysterious monsters)
  Includes index.
  ISBN 978-1-4777-7097-9 (library binding) — ISBN 978-1-4777-7098-6 (pbk.) —
  ISBN 978-1-4777-7099-3 (6-pack)
  1. Yeti—Juvenile literature. I. Title.
  QL89.2.Y4R58 2015
  001.944—dc23
                          2014001266

Manufactured in the United States of America

CPSIA Compliance Information: Batch #WS14PK8 For Further Information contact: Rosen Publishing, New York, New York at 1-800-237-9932

TABLE OF CONTENTS

What Is a Yeti?

For hundreds of years, people living in the Himalayan mountain range have reported seeing a creature they call the Yeti (also known as the Abominable Snowman). Eyewitnesses say that the Yeti walks upright like a human. However, it is much larger, has the face of an ape, and is covered in thick brown, reddish, or white fur. Over the years, hundreds of sightings have been reported.

▶ Local people have told tales of Yeti sightings for as long as anyone can remember. The first recorded accounts of the creature occurred when Europeans visited the mountains in the nineteenth century.

Half Man, Half Ape . . . or Bear

Some ancient myths describe how Yetis, which were said to be more numerous in the past, would terrorize villagers. Eventually, the villagers tricked the creatures into fighting and killing each other. The few Yetis that survived are hiding in the mountains.

Are the eyewitnesses mistaking a common animal for a Yeti? Are they just imagining it? Or is the Yeti real? Read on and see what you think.

WHERE YETI PROWLS

The Himalayas are a vast mountain range that runs through northern India, Nepal, Bhutan, Tibet, and China. They are over 1,500 miles (2,414 km) long and 100 miles (161 km) wide. The mountain range is home to some of the highest **peaks** in the world. Many are over 20,000 feet (6,096 m) above sea level.

Did You Know?

The Himalayas are still growing! The mountain range first appeared around 70 million years ago. It formed when two large, slow-moving sections of Earth's surface, called tectonic plates, collided. One of the plates continues to push up on the other one. For this reason, the Himalayas grow 0.2 inch (5 mm) taller every year.

WAY TO M.T. EVEREST B.C.

▲ The most famous Himalayan peak is Mount Everest. It is the world's tallest mountain at 29,035 feet (8,850 m).

THE PEOPLE OF THE MOUNTAINS

Himalayas is the Sanskrit word for **"abode** of snow."
The Himalayas are not an easy place to live. The huge
mountain system has varied **vegetation** and weather. The
base of the range is rainy, forested, and tropical. Other
areas are dry and rocky with very few plants. The tops of
the mountains are always frozen and covered with snow.

Because of the difficult conditions on much of the
mountain, large areas are **uninhabited**. However, every
place where people can possibly live, they do. Mountain
communities include the Sherpas in Nepal and the
Kashmirs in India.

▲ *Many communities live in sheltered
green valleys. They survive by farming,
hunting, and raising animals such as yaks,
sheep, and goats.*

THE MYSTERY BEGINS

The idea that shadowy creatures are hiding in uninhabited mountainous areas or roaming mountain passes is far from new. The Yeti has been part of local mythology and folklore for thousands of years.

The **indigenous** people both fear and worship the Yeti. The Lepcha people worshipped a Yeti-type creature as the god of the hunt. Other communities considered the apelike creature's blood to be a blessing for ceremonies. Different communities in the Himalayas tell different stories about the Yeti, but most agree that the creature does exist.

◀ *Did sightings of a strange beast lead to the creation of folktales, or did these stories lead people to imagine seeing a Yeti?*

Searching for Yeti

Some local myths hold that crossing a Yeti's path is bad luck and can even lead to instant death. The people of the mountains have been trying to avoid the creature for centuries. In contrast, outsiders who heard about the Yeti were eager to find it. The search dates back to 326 BC, when Alexander the Great asked the natives to show him the creature. They said that the Yeti could only survive at high **altitudes** and that he wouldn't be able to see it.

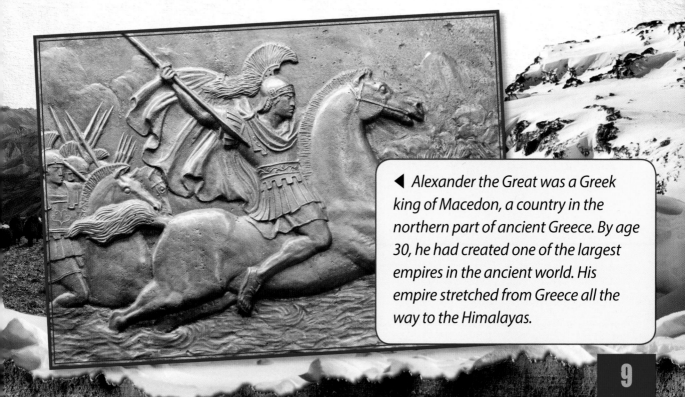

◀ *Alexander the Great was a Greek king of Macedon, a country in the northern part of ancient Greece. By age 30, he had created one of the largest empires in the ancient world. His empire stretched from Greece all the way to the Himalayas.*

First Modern Sightings

The first recorded accounts of the Yeti occurred when Europeans visited the Himalayas in the nineteenth century.

In 1832, B.H. Hodgson, a British climber visiting Nepal, reported that his guides saw a tall beast covered in hair. They said it was a Yeti. Hodgson believed that it was an orangutan.

In 1899, Lieutenant Colonel Laurence Waddell, a British explorer, reported seeing large footprints in the snow. He believed they were made by a bear, but his guides told him that a Yeti made them. Waddell remained **skeptical**.

▶ Orangutans live in the rainforests of Indonesia and Malaysia. Although they have long fur, they would not be able to survive in the cold Himalayan weather. In the Indonesian language, the word *orangutan* means "person of the forest." The word *orang means* "person" and hutan *means* "forest."

MORE ADVENTURERS, MORE SIGHTINGS

In 1925, photographer N.A. Tombazi was involved in a British geological expedition in the Himalayas at 15,000 feet (4,572 m). Tombazi saw a figure that looked human but was dark against the snow and wore no clothes. He saw the creature from 300 yards (274 m) away but wasn't fast enough to snap a picture.

On the way down, Tombazi trekked to the spot where he had seen the beast and noticed bare footprints in the snow. Each footprint clearly showed five toes. Tombazi wasn't sure what type of animal (or human) the footprints belonged to. Later, when told of the Yeti, he began to think that the prints may have belonged to the creature.

◄ Tombazi lost the trail of the creature in thick brush. Locals told him that he had seen a demon. Tombazi didn't think he had seen a demon, but he couldn't figure out what he had seen either.

Yeti Footprints

One of the biggest pieces of "evidence" is the presence of giant footprints stamped into the snowy heights of the Himalayan mountains.

In 1951, British mountaineer Eric Shipton took photos of large footprints that he saw while climbing at 20,000 feet (6,096 m) on the slopes of the Menlung Glacier. The prints, made by a two-legged animal, measured 13 inches (33 cm) wide and 18 inches (46 cm) long. Many people have examined and discussed the photos. Some argue that they are the best evidence of Yeti's existence. Others believe that the prints were made by an ordinary creature and are oddly shaped because of the way the snow melted.

▶ Eric Shipton took photos of the clearest print. He used an ice axe for scale. The footprints were fresh. Shipton followed the trail, hoping to find the creature that made them. He followed the trail for a mile (1.6 km) before it disappeared in hard ice.

What Could the Prints Be?

Some scientists argue that the footprints Shipton and others have seen could be bear prints. Others argue that bears would be moving up the mountain on four legs, leaving four prints rather than two. The prints that Shipton saw seem to belong to a biped—someone (or something) walking upright on two feet.

▲ The above footprints were made by a big brown bear. When sunlight hits the tracks, the sides often melt unevenly. The resulting footprints could look like those of some strange creature.

Could it still be a bear? Some scientists say yes. The prints could be from a bear that is "overstepping." A bear walking through snow could put its back feet into its front footprints. The resulting prints would look like the larger prints of a biped.

Or . . . perhaps they were made by a large, mysterious biped.

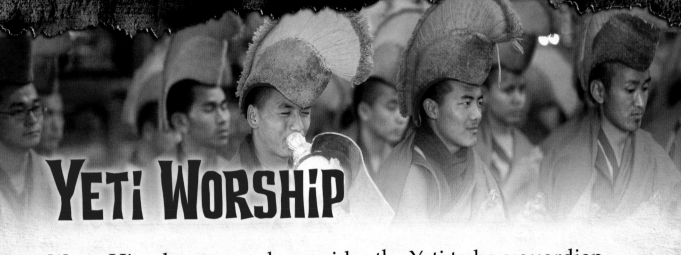

YETI WORSHIP

Many Himalayan people consider the Yeti to be a guardian of the mountains. They believe it protects the gods at the top by preventing mortals from ascending the slopes. Sherpas consider parts of the Yeti to be sacred relics.

In the town of Khumjung, a Yeti "scalp" is preserved in the local monastery. In 1960, Sir Edmund Hillary visited the remote mountain monastery in search of Yeti evidence. He was allowed to take the scalp with him to England so scientists could study it. The researchers determined that the scalp was actually crafted from the **hide** of a serow, a Himalayan goat. To this day, however, the people of Khumjung keep the object under lock and key in the monastery and still consider it to be sacred.

▲ *Local people hold the scalp in high regard as a good luck charm. Sir Edmund Hillary had a lot of trouble getting it out. The villagers believed that bad luck would befall the village if the scalp left.*

Mani Rimdu Festival

Mani Rimdu is the most important festival of the Sherpa people. It is held each fall in eastern Nepal.

The Yeti always plays a role in the event. During ritual dances, monks wear masks and portray divine beings. One dancer, posing as a Yeti, wears a headdress of skin and hair that symbolizes a Yeti scalp. The scalp is said to be sacred. The dancer represents the spirit of the Yeti, which has been sent by the gods to punish people for their sins. During the ritual, the participants drive the Yeti spirit—and evil—out of the village.

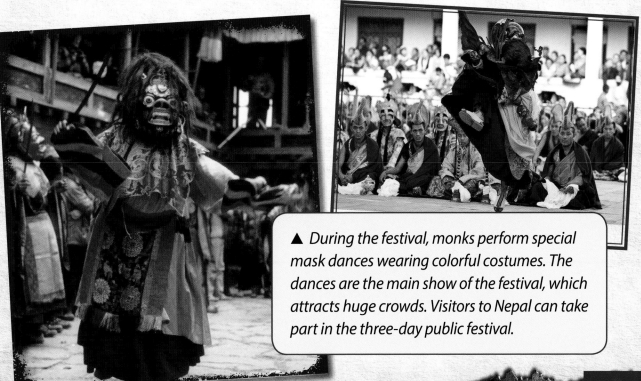

▲ *During the festival, monks perform special mask dances wearing colorful costumes. The dances are the main show of the festival, which attracts huge crowds. Visitors to Nepal can take part in the three-day public festival.*

YETi EXPEDiTiONS

In 1954, the London Daily Mail newspaper paid for an expedition to the Himalayas to prove whether or not the Yeti exists. During the trip, scientists took footprint photos and brought home samples of hair from a "Yeti." They analyzed the hair under a microscope and compared it to the hair of other animals. They were unable to figure out which animal the hair belonged to, but they believed that it came from a hoofed creature.

▲ *The picture above shows the members of the 1954 Daily Mail Abominable Snowman Expedition to the Himalayas. The team was made up of several respected scientists and many Sherpas. Although the expedition never recovered a Yeti, it did track several trails of footprints identical to those photographed by Shipton.*

The Mountaineer on the Hunt

After climbing Everest in 1953 and seeing strange footprints, Sir Edmund Hillary wanted to learn the truth about the Yeti. In 1960, he and 22 scientists embarked on an expedition sponsored by the heads of the World Book Encyclopedia.

Hillary and his team took scientific equipment as well as special cameras. The team searched the mountains for 10 months looking for scientific evidence of the Yeti. They did not have much luck in their search. Even with all their special equipment, they came up empty.

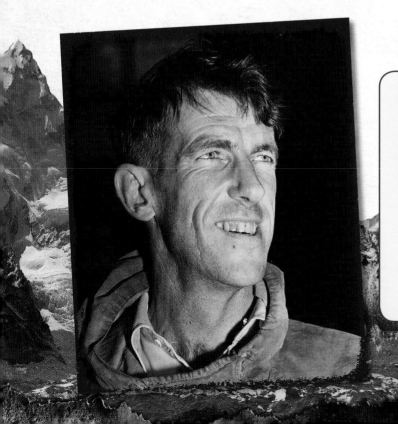

◄ Sir Edmund Hillary's scientific equipment included trip-wire cameras, which were set to take a photo if someone (or something) touched a wire set across a trail. The team also used time-lapse photography, which can capture movement that can't normally be seen by the human eye. Infrared cameras gathered images at night.

BONES, HAiR, AND DNA

As scientific technology has advanced, previously unexplainable pieces of "evidence" have been explained. The **DNA** taken from an unknown animal can be compared to the codes of known animals. This technology has been valuable to Yeti researchers.

In 2008, curators at the Royal College of Surgeons Museum in London cataloged a collection left to the museum by primatologist and **cryptozoologist** William Charles Osman Hill. In the collection was a mummified finger 3.5 inches (8.9 cm) long and 1 inch (2.5 cm) thick in a box marked "Yeti's finger." Apparently, the finger had been taken from a Yeti hand found in a temple in Nepal. DNA analysis in 2011 proved that the finger was human.

▲ The finger came from the "Pangboche Hand," an artifact from a Buddhist monastery in Pangboche, Nepal. Monks in the monastery claimed that the hand was from a Yeti.

THE LATEST DNA FINDINGS

Most recently, in 2013, Professor Bryan Sykes of the **esteemed** University of Oxford in the United Kingdom conducted DNA research. He found a match between two samples thought to be Yeti hairs and an ancient animal.

Sykes compared the "Yeti hair" to DNA from other animals. The hair was a perfect match with a sample from an ancient polar bear jawbone from Norway. The jawbone dates to between 40,000 and 120,000 years ago. Sykes believes that the "Yeti" may actually be a descendant of the ancient polar bear or a **hybrid** of a brown bear and a polar bear.

▶ *The habitat range of prehistoric bears stretched across Europe and all the way to Asia. Did some bears survive to this day in the Himalayas? Sykes wonders if perhaps these bears walk on two feet more often than typical bears, which could explain Yeti sightings.*

SCIENTIFIC VIEW

Most scientists believe that the Yeti, in the form of a human-ape hybrid, is a myth. It would be difficult for any animal to live as high up in the mountains as "Yeti footprints" have been found because of the cold, low oxygen levels, and lack of food.

Scientists also suggest that many logical explanations exist for Yeti sightings and "evidence." And speaking of evidence, there hasn't been as much as might be expected if such a creature lived in the mountains: bodies, bones, or teeth, for example. What hard evidence has been found—footprints, finger bones, hair, and scalps—has been otherwise explained by science.

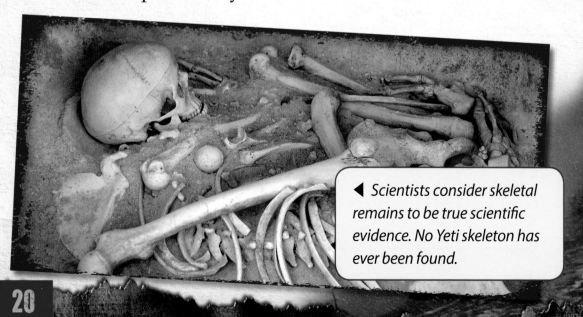

◀ Scientists consider skeletal remains to be true scientific evidence. No Yeti skeleton has ever been found.

Yeti Sightings Explained

What about all the sightings? Seeing the Yeti while at high altitudes may be explained by **hallucinations** caused by lack of oxygen. An oxygen-deprived brain can imagine many interesting things. At lower altitudes, sightings may be a case of people seeing what they expect to see. They are looking for the Yeti, so they may see its form in a more common animal. In other words, they are misidentifying animals like monkeys or bears.

Some Yeti sightings may also be **hoaxes** or pranks. This makes scientists even more skeptical.

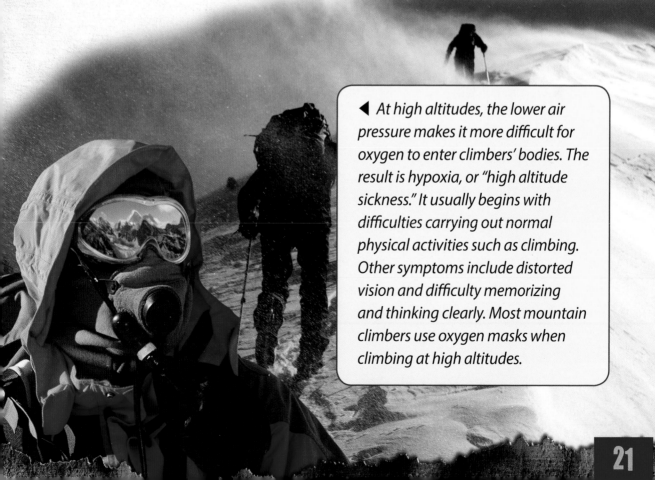

◄ At high altitudes, the lower air pressure makes it more difficult for oxygen to enter climbers' bodies. The result is hypoxia, or "high altitude sickness." It usually begins with difficulties carrying out normal physical activities such as climbing. Other symptoms include distorted vision and difficulty memorizing and thinking clearly. Most mountain climbers use oxygen masks when climbing at high altitudes.

NOT CONVINCED BY SCIENCE

The number of people who believe in the Yeti has declined. Yet even in the Himalayas, many are still convinced of the creature's existence, regardless of scientific data.

Many groups of indigenous Himalayan peoples both fear and worship the Yeti. They consider the Yeti to be holy and do not welcome people questioning its existence.

The Sakteng Wildlife Sanctuary is a national park in Bhutan. It was created in 2003 to preserve wildlife, including the Yeti (known in the area as Migoi). The people of Bhutan consider the Migoi to have great strength, magical powers, and invisibility.

▶ Science has proven that some Yeti relics actually belong to other animals. Yet the creature may still exist. An unknown animal may be lurking in the mountains. The Himalayas are vast and mostly unexplored. If only a small number of Yetis were alive, and if they mainly hunted at night, they would be even more difficult to find.

THE SIGHTINGS CONTINUE

Today, a healthy tourist industry exists in Himalayan regions like Tibet. More than 3,500 people have climbed Mount Everest. In 2012, 234 climbers reached the peak. Sightings of the Yeti continue. Both climbers and Sherpas still claim to see the creature every now and then. Could they all be wrong?

▲ *Some claim that animals could never survive as high up as Yetis have been found. However, it's been noted that yaks climb to over 16,000 feet (4,877 m).*

▶ *Sherpas often work as guides for mountain-climbing expeditions. They also help carry heavy loads of climbing equipment and supplies.*

23

WHO OR WHAT COULD YETI BE?

Many believe that the Yeti is actually a bear.

Reinhold Messner was a mountain climber who made the first solo ascent of Everest without extra oxygen, In 1986, Messner claimed to have come face-to-face with a Yeti. He was on a long trek at the time, trying to follow a Sherpa route from centuries ago. As he climbed a steep slope, he saw a large, dark, furry figure on the trail. The creature, which had long arms and short legs, was running, faster than humanly possible, in and out of the trees . . . on two feet. Messner says he saw the animal from as close as 30 feet (9 m) away. At the time, he believed it was a Yeti and spent over a **decade** searching for the beast.

◀ Years later, Reinhold Messner concluded that he'd really seen a brown bear, which can walk both upright and on all fours. But did he really see a bear? Bears can stand and even walk on two feet, but when they run fast, they use all four legs.

PREHISTORIC TIES?

Those who claim to have seen a Yeti often describe it as having the face of an ape. Could the Yeti be a descendant of apes or prehistoric humans? Perhaps it is a creature that has adapted to the harsh conditions of the Himalayas over time.

In the 1950s, zoologist Bernard Heuvelmans suggested that Yeti footprints might have been made by a descendant of *Gigantopithecus*, a huge ape that lived in China and India 12 million years ago. In the 1980s, other researchers claimed that the Yeti could be a descendant of Neanderthals. Not many scientists agree with either **hypothesis**.

▶ Neanderthals are an extinct species of humans that used tools made of bones, antlers, and wood. They were hunters who could kill animals as large as mammoths, extinct relatives of elephants.

YETI'S COUSINS?

The Himalayas aren't the only place where unexplained creatures have been said to roam. Similar mysterious beings have been reported on every continent except Antarctica.

In the United States, thousands of people have claimed to see Bigfoot (also known as Sasquatch), a large apelike creature that bears a striking resemblance to Yeti. In fact, Bigfoot might even be more famous than Yeti. It has been spotted from Maine to California. Every year, dozens of people claim to have seen the creature. Some have even presented video, footprints, and hair evidence. Most scientists assert, as they do with the Yeti, that Bigfoot is not real. And just like with the Yeti, they will never convince believers.

◀ *Sasquatch sightings have been reported in every US state except Hawaii. Outside of North America, there's the Yowie in Australia, the Xucren of China, and the Hibagon of Japan, to name just a few.*

The Alma in Russia

In Russia, stories of a large apelike creature named the Alma go back for centuries. The creature's description is similar to that of the Yeti, but the Alma is said to appear more human. While it looks like a hairy human, the Alma has superhuman abilities in that it can run and swim faster than any person. The Alma, an **omnivore**, is reported to live with its mate in holes in the ground.

Sightings of the Alma have been recorded since 1881. In 1937, Russian soldiers shot and killed two Almas. Because of the war, the corpses could not be properly examined scientifically. Since then, expeditions to find the Alma have been unsuccessful. However, Alma sightings have become more common over the past two decades, so the proof may be coming soon to a science lab near you.

◄ *Almas look more like hairy humans than apes. Witnesses described Almas as about 6 feet (1.8 m) tall with flat noses, weak chins, large eyebrows, and bodies covered with reddish-brown hair. Alma means "wild man" in the Mongolian language.*

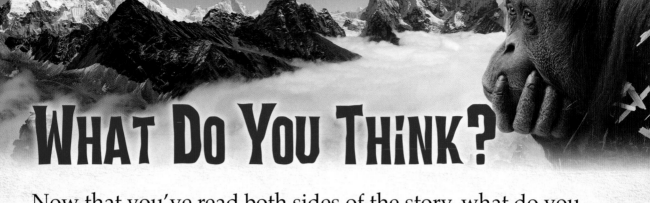

WHAT DO YOU THINK?

Now that you've read both sides of the story, what do you believe? Is it possible that the Yeti exists somewhere in the hidden reaches of the Himalayas, or has it all been a case of mistaken identity?

One thing is certain. The story of the Yeti has been interesting and entertaining, stirring people's imaginations for many years. The Yeti is big business in Nepal. Many tourists head to the area with an interest in the strange stories. Stamps, mugs, and T-shirts feature the Yeti's image. There is even a hotel named the Yak and Yeti.

▲ More and more tourists visit the Himalayas and Nepal every year. Some come for the natural beauty, while others come to search for the Yeti.

WORLDWIDE FAME

The Yeti has made its mark outside of the Himalayas, too. The Abominable Snowman has been featured in TV shows, such as *Scooby Doo*, books, movies, and video games. The Disney World attraction called Expedition Everest features a 25 foot (7.6 m) tall robotic Yeti.

Interest in the creature will not die down, no matter what evidence science has to offer. As long as there are still areas to be explored in the mountains, there will be adventurers who will chase their secrets. Who knows what they will find?

EYEWITNESS TALE

In 1998, American climber Craig Calonica claimed to have seen two Yetis after skiing on Everest. He described them as having thick, shiny black fur and walking upright. They were 6 feet (1.8 m) tall and had long arms and huge hands. He told the press, "I saw something that was not human, that was not a gorilla, not a deer, not a goat and not a bear."

▶ *The Yeti is quite popular in the world of comics, too, although the character is sometimes portrayed as a real monster. It is probably fine with the Yeti. It does not read comics. Or does it?*

GLOSSARY

abode (uh-BOHD) The place where someone lives.

altitudes (AL-tuh-toodz) The height of something (such as an airplane) above sea level.

coined (KOIND) Created a new word or phrase that other people begin to use.

cryptozoologist (KRIP-tow-zoh-ah-luh-jist) Someone who studies and searches for animals who may or may not exist.

decade (DEH-kayd) A period of 10 years.

depictions (dih-PIKT-shunz) Images or words that represent someone or something.

DNA (DEE IN AY) A substance that carries genetic information in the cells of plants and animals.

esteemed (ih-STEEMD) Respected and admired.

hallucinations (huh-loo-shuh-NAY-shunz) Experiences of images, sounds, smells, or other things that seem real but that do not really exist.

hide (HYD) The skin of an animal.

hoaxes (HOHKS-ez) Acts meant to trick people into believing or accepting as genuine things that are false and often preposterous.

hybrid (HY-brud) An animal or plant that is an offspring of two different kinds of animals or plants.

hypothesis (hy-PAH-theh-ses) Something believed to be true but requiring further investigation for proof that it is.

indigenous (in-DIH-jeh-nus) Produced, living, growing, or occurring naturally in a certain region or environment.

omnivore (OM-nih-vawr) An animal that eats both plants and animals.

peaks (PEEKS) The pointed tops of mountains.

skeptical (SKEP-ti-kul) Having or expressing doubt, either in general or about a certain statement or topic.

uninhabited (un-in-HA-but-ed) Not settled or lived in by people.

vegetation (veh-jih-TAY-shun) The plants that live in a certain area.

FOR MORE INFORMATION

FURTHER READING

Colson, Mary. *Bigfoot and the Yeti*. Solving Mysteries with Science. Mankato, MN: Capstone Press, 2014.

Rajczak, Kristen. *Climbing Mount Everest*. Thrill Seekers. New York: Gareth Stevens, 2014.

Sheehan, Robert. *Conquering Mount Everest*. Discovery Education: Sensational True Stories. New York: PowerKids Press, 2013.

WEBSITES

Due to the changing nature of Internet links, PowerKids Press has developed an online list of websites related to the subject of this book. This site is updated regularly. Please use this link to access the list:

www.powerkidslinks.com/mymo/yeti/

INDEX